THIS BOOK BELONGS TO

_____

FOR THE KIDS WHO WANT TO
MEET SANTA

ISBN: 9798894581873

IT WAS CHRISTMAS EVE AT THE NORTH POLE, AND SANTA'S WORKSHOP BUZZED WITH EXCITEMENT. THE ELVES WERE WORKING HARD, WRAPPING GIFTS, CHECKING LISTS, AND PREPARING FOR THE BIGGEST NIGHT OF THE YEAR.

BUT IN A DARK CORNER, JINX, THE SMALLEST OF THE ELVES, WAS GLARING AT
THE ACTIVITY AROUND HIM. HE HAD ALWAYS BEEN OVERLOOKED, LEFT BEHIND.
IT WASN'T FAIR. WHY DIDN'T ANYONE APPRECIATE ALL THE HARD WORK
HE PUT IN? THIS YEAR, HE DECIDED THINGS WOULD CHANGE.

JINX HAD A PLAN—A TERRIBLE PLAN. HE WOULD STEAL THE MASTER KEY,
THE KEY TO ALL CHRISTMAS MAGIC. WITH IT, HE COULD CONTROL SANTA'S SLEIGH,
STOP THE GIFTS FROM BEING DELIVERED, AND RUIN CHRISTMAS FOR EVERYONE.

SNEAKING THROUGH THE WORKSHOP AT NIGHT, JINX MADE HIS MOVE.
THE MASTER KEY WAS KEPT IN A VAULT HIDDEN DEEP INSIDE THE WORKSHOP.
NO ONE KNEW HOW TO ACCESS IT EXCEPT SANTA AND A FEW TRUSTED ELVES.

BUT JINX HAD DONE HIS HOMEWORK. USING A SPECIAL SPELL HE'D LEARNED IN SECRET,
HE UNLOCKED THE VAULT AND GRABBED THE GLOWING MASTER KEY.
"THIS IS MINE NOW," HE WHISPERED TO HIMSELF.

BY THE TIME JACK AND MIA, TWO OF SANTA'S TRUSTED HELPERS, NOTICED THE KEY WAS MISSING, IT WAS ALREADY TOO LATE. SANTA RUSHED IN, HIS FACE GRIM. " JINX HAS TAKEN THE KEY," HE SAID. "WITHOUT IT, CHRISTMAS WILL BE IN GRAVE DANGER."

MIA CLENCHED HER FISTS. "WE HAVE TO STOP HIM."

SANTA HANDED THEM A MAP. "FOLLOW THIS TRAIL THROUGH THE MOUNTAINS. JINX IS HIDING SOMEWHERE THERE. BUT HURRY, TIME IS RUNNING OUT."

JACK AND MIA GRABBED THEIR GEAR AND HEADED OUT INTO THE COLD, THEIR HEARTS RACING. THEY COULDN'T LET JINX DESTROY CHRISTMAS. THE SNOWY LANDSCAPE STRETCHED BEFORE THEM, THE WIND HOWLING THROUGH THE TREES.

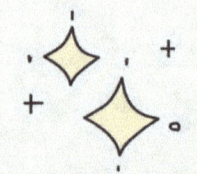

HOURS PASSED, THE JOURNEY TREACHEROUS, BUT THEY PRESSED ON. THE DEEPER THEY WENT INTO THE MOUNTAINS, THE MORE THEY FELT JINX'S MAGIC WEAKENING THE VERY AIR AROUND THEM. THE PATH AHEAD GREW DARK, FILLED WITH SHADOWS AND STRANGE NOISES.

FINALLY, THEY REACHED A HIDDEN CAVE. THE FAINT GLOW OF THE MASTER KEY COULD BE SEEN FROM THE ENTRANCE. THEY HAD FOUND HIM.

"BE CAREFUL," JACK WHISPERED. "THIS IS IT."

INSIDE THE CAVE, JINX STOOD IN FRONT OF A MASSIVE STONE DOOR, THE MASTER KEY FLOATING IN HIS HANDS. HE TURNED AND GRINNED WHEN HE SAW THEM. "WELL, WELL. IF IT ISN'T THE HEROES. YOU'RE TOO LATE, THOUGH."

"YOU CAN'T WIN, JINX," MIA SAID, STEPPING FORWARD. "GIVE US THE KEY!"

JINX LAUGHED DARKLY. "NOT SO FAST. IF YOU WANT THE KEY, YOU'LL HAVE TO SOLVE MY CHALLENGES. THREE OF THEM. FAIL, AND CHRISTMAS IS OVER."

JINX RAISED HIS HAND, AND THE FIRST CHALLENGE APPEARED ON THE WALL:

"I HAVE KEYS BUT OPEN NO DOORS.

I HAVE SPACE BUT NO ROOMS.

WHAT AM I?"

JACK SCRATCHED HIS HEAD. "HMM. THAT'S A TOUGH ONE."

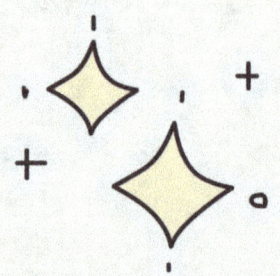

MIA THOUGHT FOR A MOMENT, THEN SMILED. "A KEYBOARD! IT HAS KEYS, BUT DOESN'T OPEN ANY DOORS."

JINX'S FACE TWISTED IN FRUSTRATION. "NO MATTER! THE NEXT ONE WILL BE HARDER!"

THE SECOND CHALLENGE APPEARED:
"I CAN BE CRACKED,
I CAN BE MADE,
I CAN BE TOLD,
I CAN BE PLAYED.
WHAT AM I?"

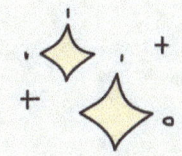

MIA BLINKED, THINKING HARD. "A JOKE!" SHE SAID. "A JOKE CAN BE
CRACKED, MADE, TOLD, AND PLAYED!"

JINX SCOWLED. "YOU'RE TOO CLEVER. BUT YOU HAVEN'T WON YET."

THE FINAL CHALLENGE APPEARED ON THE WALL:
"THE MORE YOU TAKE,
THE MORE YOU LEAVE BEHIND.
WHAT AM I?"

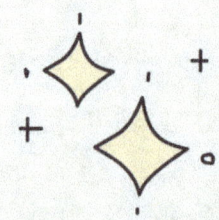

JACK LOOKED AT THE RIDDLE, PUZZLED. "THIS ONE'S TRICKY..."

MIA'S EYES LIT UP. "FOOTSTEPS! THE MORE YOU TAKE, THE MORE YOU LEAVE BEHIND."

JINX SLAMMED HIS FIST AGAINST THE STONE WALL. "THIS ISN'T POSSIBLE! YOU SOLVED THEM ALL!"

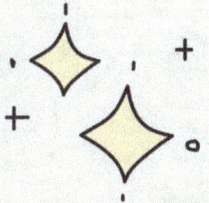

THE MASTER KEY HOVERED IN FRONT OF JACK, ITS GLOW PULSING. JINX TRIED TO STOP THEM, BUT THE POWER OF THE KEY WAS TOO MUCH FOR HIM.

JACK REACHED OUT AND TOOK THE KEY. THE MOMENT HIS FINGERS TOUCHED IT,
A FLASH OF LIGHT FILLED THE CAVE, AND JINX'S DARK MAGIC BEGAN TO UNRAVEL.

JINX STAGGERED BACK, HIS EYES WIDE WITH PANIC. "NO... THIS ISN'T HOW IT WAS SUPPOSED TO END."

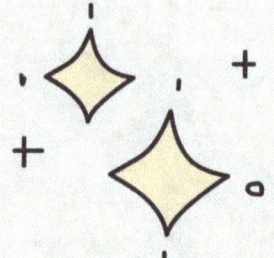

JACK AND MIA STOOD TALL, THE POWER OF CHRISTMAS SWIRLING AROUND THEM.
JINX'S PLANS WERE FALLING APART.

"YOU'VE LOST, JINX," MIA SAID GENTLY.

JINX DROPPED TO HIS KNEES, DEFEATED. "I THOUGHT... I THOUGHT RUINING CHRISTMAS WOULD MAKE PEOPLE NOTICE ME."

JACK SHOOK HIS HEAD. "CHRISTMAS ISN'T ABOUT BEING NOTICED. IT'S ABOUT KINDNESS, SHARING, AND TOGETHERNESS."

JINX LOOKED DOWN AT THE GROUND, ASHAMED. "I... I'M SORRY. I WAS SELFISH AND ANGRY. I NEVER WANTED TO HURT ANYONE."

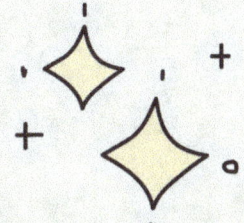

SANTA APPEARED IN THE DOORWAY OF THE CAVE, HIS FACE WARM. "JINX, EVERYONE FEELS LEFT OUT SOMETIMES. BUT HURTING OTHERS ISN'T THE ANSWER."

JINX NODDED, HIS HEAD HANGING LOW. "I WAS WRONG. I DIDN'T REALIZE HOW IMPORTANT CHRISTMAS REALLY IS."

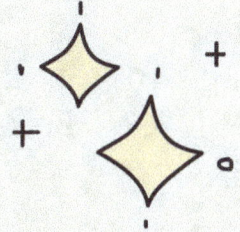

SANTA STEPPED FORWARD, PLACING A HAND ON JINX'S SHOULDER. "YOU'VE LEARNED AN IMPORTANT LESSON, JINX. CHRISTMAS ISN'T ABOUT BEING THE CENTER OF ATTENTION. IT'S ABOUT SPREADING JOY TO OTHERS."

JINX LOOKED UP, A SMALL BUT GENUINE SMILE FORMING. "I'LL NEVER FORGET THIS. THANK YOU, SANTA."

SANTA SMILED BACK. "YOU'RE ALWAYS PART OF THE NORTH POLE FAMILY, JINX."

WITH THE MASTER KEY NOW SAFELY RETURNED, JACK AND MIA HELPED SANTA DELIVER THE FINAL GIFTS. CHRISTMAS WAS BACK ON TRACK.

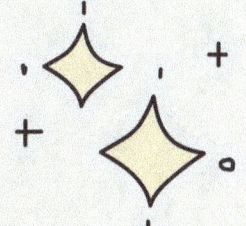

AS THE SLEIGH FLEW ACROSS THE WORLD, JACK AND MIA WATCHED THE
SNOW-COVERED TOWNS BELOW, FILLED WITH THE MAGIC OF CHRISTMAS MORNING.

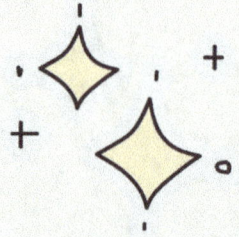

BACK AT THE NORTH POLE, THE ELVES CHEERED. "CHRISTMAS IS SAVED!"

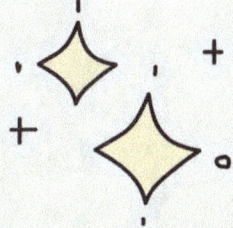

JINX STOOD QUIETLY, WATCHING THEM FROM A DISTANCE. HE HAD LEARNED A VALUABLE LESSON ABOUT CHRISTMAS, AND ABOUT HIMSELF.

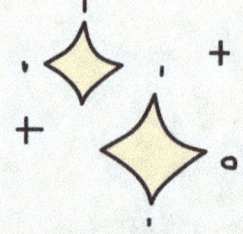

SANTA'S SLEIGH RETURNED TO THE NORTH POLE, AND JACK AND MIA WERE PRAISED FOR THEIR BRAVERY. "YOU SAVED CHRISTMAS!" THE ELVES SHOUTED.

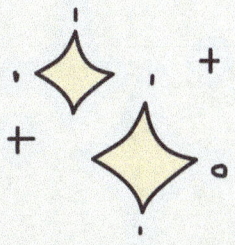

JINX, HUMBLED, STOOD AT THE EDGE OF THE CELEBRATION. HE WASN'T ANGRY ANYMORE. HE HAD LEARNED THE TRUE MEANING OF CHRISTMAS.

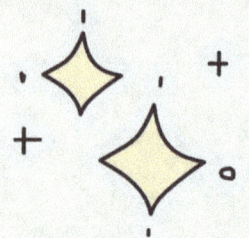

"I'LL ALWAYS BE A PART OF THIS," HE WHISPERED TO HIMSELF.

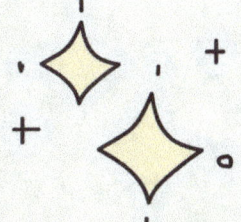

JACK AND MIA SMILED, KNOWING THEY HAD MADE THE WORLD
A LITTLE BRIGHTER.

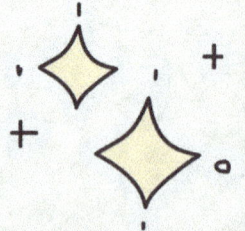

AND AS THE NIGHT SKY SPARKLED WITH CHRISTMAS MAGIC, THEY ALL
KNEW THAT THE SPIRIT OF CHRISTMAS WOULD LAST FOREVER.

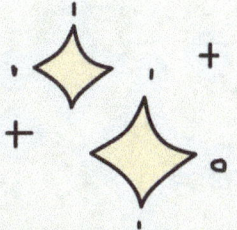

JINX, NOW AT PEACE, JOINED THE OTHERS. "MERRY CHRISTMAS,"
HE SAID, TRULY MEANING IT.

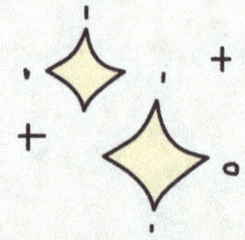

AND SO, THE MAGIC OF CHRISTMAS LIVED ON, NOT THROUGH CONTROL, BUT THROUGH LOVE, KINDNESS, AND THE JOY OF SHARING.

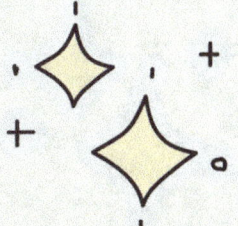

THE SLEIGH SOARED THROUGH THE NIGHT SKY, THE WORLD BELOW
GLOWING WITH THE WARMTH OF THE HOLIDAY SEASON.

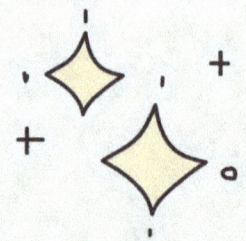

JINX LOOKED OUT OVER THE SNOWY LANDSCAPE, FINALLY AT PEACE WITH HIMSELF. HE HAD LEARNED THAT THE REAL MAGIC WAS IN GIVING, NOT TAKING.

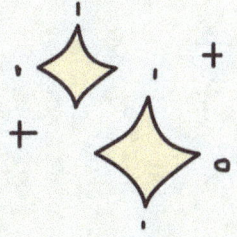

SANTA'S VOICE ECHOED IN THE DISTANCE. "MERRY CHRISTMAS TO ALL,
AND TO ALL A GOOD NIGHT!"

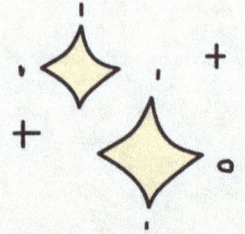

AND WITH THAT, CHRISTMAS WAS SAFE ONCE MORE. THE NORTH POLE WAS FILLED WITH WARMTH, JOY, AND THE MAGIC OF THE SEASON.

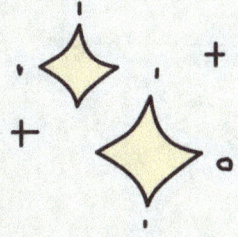

EVERYONE KNEW THAT THIS CHRISTMAS WAS SPECIAL—NOT BECAUSE OF THE GIFTS, BUT BECAUSE THEY HAD LEARNED THE TRUE MEANING OF CHRISTMAS TOGETHER.

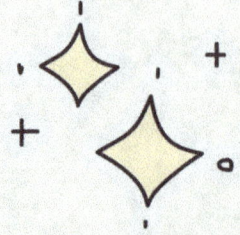

I HOPE YOU LIKED THIS BOOK. PLEASE CHECK OUT MY OTHER BOOKS.

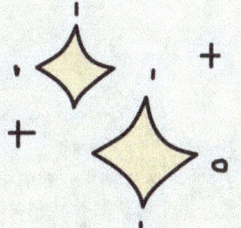

www.ingramcontent.com/pod-product-compliance
Lightning Source LLC
Chambersburg PA
CBHW081540120626
46550CB00009B/2803